Children of
PUERTO RICO

THE WORLD'S CHILDREN

Children of
PUERTO RICO

MICHAEL ELSOHN ROSS
PHOTOGRAPHS BY FELIX RIGAU

Carolrhoda Books, Inc./Minneapolis

To the children of Puerto Rico

We wish to acknowledge the help of the families and teachers of the children shown in this book for all their cooperation and enthusiasm. Muchas gracias.

Text copyright © 2002 by Michael Elsohn Ross
Photographs copyright © 2002 by Felix Rigau
Additional photographs used with permission of: Knights of Columbus Headquarters Museum, p. 8; Independent Picture Service, p. 9 (top); New York Public Library, p. 10 (bottom); © Thomas R. Fletcher, p. 21 (bottom); © Tony Arruza, p. 29 (left). Illustration on page 7 copyright © 2002 by Carolrhoda Books, Inc.

Carolrhoda Books, Inc.
A division of Lerner Publishing Group
241 First Avenue North
Minneapolis, MN 55401 U.S.A.

Website address: www.lernerbooks.com

LIBRARY OF CONGRESS CATALOGING-IN-PUBLICATION DATA

Ross, Michael Elsohn, 1952–
    Children of Puerto Rico / by Michael Elsohn Ross; photographs by Felix Rigau.
       p.   cm. — (The world's children)
    Includes index.
    ISBN 1-57505-522-8 (lib. bdg. : alk. paper)
    1. Puerto Rico—Social life and customs—Juvenile literature. 2. Children—Puerto Rico—social life and customs—Juvenile literature. [1. Puerto Rico—Social life and customs.] I. Rigau, Felix, ill. II. Title. III. World's children (Minneapolis, Minn.)
F1960 .R67 2002
072.9505'3—dc21   2001-000514

Manufactured in the United States of America
1 2 3 4 5 6 – JR – 07 06 05 04 03 02

Finding a place to watch the ocean is easy in Puerto Rico. It's a tropical island. Located about 1,000 miles southeast of Florida, Puerto Rico is 100 miles long and 35 miles wide—about the size of Connecticut. It has many miles of coast along the Atlantic Ocean and the Caribbean Sea.

To see the Atlantic, Tatiana likes to go to an old fort named El Morro. It's in San Juan, Puerto Rico's biggest city and capital. From the fort's high walls, Tatiana can see the vastness of the sea. The ships in San Juan's harbor look small from this distance. But they are really much bigger than the ships used by Christopher Columbus.

Columbus arrived in this same harbor in 1493. He was on his second expedition for Spain. The Taíno people, a group of Arawak Indians, were the island's only inhabitants then.

Above: *Tatiana likes to visit the old fort El Morro.*
Right: *Many large ships use the busy harbor at San Juan, the capital city of Puerto Rico.*

ATLANTIC OCEAN

Aquadilla
Arecibo
San Juan
Bayamón
Carolina
Loíza
Luquillo
CULEBRA ISLAND
Caguana
Dewey
PUERTO RICO
Caguas
EL YUNQUE
Mayagüez
Maricao
VIEQUES ISLAND
CORDILLERA CENTRAL
Sabana Grande
Ponce
Guayama
to MONA ISLAND
CABO ROJO
Guánica

CARIBBEAN SEA

Miles
0   10   20   30
0   10 20 30 40
Kilometers

N

UNITED STATES
Florida
ATLANTIC OCEAN
BAHAMAS
DOMINICAN REPUBLIC
CUBA
WEST INDIES
VIRGIN ISLANDS
JAMAICA
HAITI
Mona Island
LESSER ANTILLES
COMMONWEALTH OF PUERTO RICO
CARIBBEAN SEA
SOUTH AMERICA

Columbus called the people he met in Puerto Rico "Indians" because he thought he was in India. Puerto Rico and other islands in the area were later called the West Indies.

The Taíno showed Columbus some gold nuggets they had found on the island. Columbus expected that Spain could find more gold on the island someday.

The Spaniards returned 15 years later. Led by Ponce de León, they built a settlement that came to be called Puerto Rico, which means "rich port." Later the whole island was called Puerto Rico.

Puerto Rico was not always called Puerto Rico. Christopher Columbus called it San Juan Bautista (after Saint John the Baptist). The Taíno people called it Borinquén (which means "land of a noble lord").

The Spaniards had guns and the Taíno did not. The Spaniards easily seized the land where the Taíno grew beans, squash, and other crops. They forced the Taíno to help them farm and look for gold. In 1511, the Taíno revolted. The Spaniards killed most of them. Some fled to other islands. Only a few remained on Puerto Rico.

Two years later, the Spaniards began enslaving people from Africa. The Spanish mines quickly ran out of gold. Instead of mining for gold, these slaves worked on plantations growing sugarcane, coffee, and tobacco.

Gidalys lives in San Juan. She likes to fly kites with her father and hear his stories about the days when Spanish ships sailed across the Atlantic to start new colonies in Central and South America. Puerto Rico was the first large island these ships reached after leaving Spain. They often stopped at San Juan for repairs and supplies.

Left: *Spanish settlers forced the Taíno people to work for them.*
Below: *Gidalys and her father visit El Morro, a historic park, almost every week.*

Right: *Standing high above the harbor, El Morro once helped protect San Juan from pirates and from the ships of other nations.* Below: *A pirate ship attacks another ship.*

Caca Fogo.   *Caca Plata.*

Other European nations were also settling Central and South America. Since San Juan was an important stopping place, their troops sometimes tried to seize the city. In addition, pirates plundered ships in the harbor. Some-times Puerto Rican pirates, such as Miguel Henríquez, terrorized English and French ships. To protect San Juan, the Spanish built a series of large forts. The largest was El Morro. It had many cannons and walls 150 feet high.

Spain ruled Puerto Rico until 1898. Then Spain lost the Spanish-American War and gave the United States control of Puerto Rico. Modern Puerto Rico is still part of the United States. It is a commonwealth territory. The Commonwealth of Puerto Rico includes the main island and many nearby smaller islands.

Puerto Rico's shores have many beautiful beaches.

About three and a half million people live in Puerto Rico. They have many of the rights of U.S. citizens. But citizens in a commonwealth don't have all the rights of citizens in a state. For example, Puerto Ricans can't vote in U.S. presidential elections.

Many traditions from the Spaniards, the Taíno, and the African slaves still survive in Puerto Rico. The island's official languages are English and Spanish. But Taíno words such as *canoe, hammock, barbecue,* and *hurricane* are used every day in Puerto Rico and throughout the world.

Like Joumor (left) *and Wilomaris* (right), *most children in Puerto Rico are descended from early Spanish, Taíno, and African people.*

The Spaniards introduced Spanish music and architecture. They also brought their religion, Catholicism, to the island. Many modern Puerto Ricans are Catholics.

San Juan has lots of modern buildings. But it also has buildings that date from Spanish colonial days. Some of the oldest buildings are found in a neighborhood called Old San Juan.

Many buildings in Puerto Rico show the influence of Spanish architecture. Modern San Juan also has fast-food restaurants, shopping centers, and chain stores.

In another neighborhood, vendors set up open-air shops on a busy shopping street. Baby Luis spends lots of time at his parents' fruit stand. When his mother works at the stand, she brings him along with her.

Many people stop at the stand to buy *plátanos* and other fruits. *Plátanos* are a type of banana. For many Puerto Ricans, cooked *plátanos* are an important part of the daily *comida,* the meal served at midday.

To sell his *plátanos*, Luis's father calls out, *"Plátanos, dos por peso."* Puerto Ricans use U.S. coins and paper money, but they call the dollar a *peso*. So Luis's father's *plátanos* are two for one dollar.

Baby Luis's mother (opposite page) *and father sell fruit from a fruit stand to customers like this man* (right). *In many parts of Puerto Rico, people can pick fruits such as mangos, papaya, tamarindo, and guava from trees growing along the road.*

Near San Juan is the town of Loíza. It was settled by African slaves who earned their freedom. Most of them became Catholics. They built the small Church of the Holy Spirit and St. Patrick. Joshua and Joelly live near Loíza, and they come to town often to shop with their mother. They pass the old church, which is still being used 350 years after it was built.

Each July, people in Loíza hold a special festival called *fiestas de Santiago.* It blends their Catholic traditions with African dances, costumes, and other customs.

Joshua and Joelly (above) *often pass by the Church of the Holy Spirit and St. Patrick* (below).

Eduar (left) *rides his friend's horse through the waves. He and his sisters* (above) *don't have a horse, but they do have rabbits, chickens, and parakeets.*

Eduar's family lives near Loíza. Puerto Rico is always warm, so Eduar and his friends can swim all year round. They also like to snorkel and ride the waves on their boogie boards (small surfboards). A friend of Eduar's owns a horse, and sometimes Eduar rides the horse along the shore.

Eduar's family, including grandparents, aunts, uncles, and cousins, all live next to each other in three houses nestled side by side. The family eats lots of seafoods such as fish, shrimp, and conches. They gather these foods themselves. They also collect coconuts for their sweet-tasting milk and meat.

A few miles away, Joseph and his baseball team are competing in the local Little League playoffs. The boys speak mostly Spanish, but they sprinkle in English words, such as "strike," "inning," and "bases."

Baseball is the most popular sport in Puerto Rico. The island doesn't have a major league team, but it sends many players to the American and National leagues in the United States. Joseph's favorite player is Roberto Alomar. Joseph has a great pitching arm and dreams of playing for the New York Yankees someday.

By the final inning, Joseph has struck out seven batters, and his team is ahead. The next batter hits a ground

Joseph dreams of playing for the New York Yankees someday.

Left: *Joseph's team
celebrates when Joseph
strikes out a batter.*
Above: *El Yunque is
one of the wettest
places in Puerto Rico.*

ball. One of Joseph's teammates throws it to first base in time to make a third out. It's a victory for Joseph's team.

As the game ends, it begins to rain. Rain falls often in parts of Puerto Rico, especially in the island's rain forests. The largest rain forest is southwest of Loíza, on the slopes of a mountain called El Yunque. Almost every morning, clouds build up around the highest slopes of the mountain. By afternoon, it begins to drizzle. Before long, there is a heavy rain. El Yunque is soaked by about 200 inches of rain a year.

El Yunque is part of the Caribbean National Forest, the only rain forest in the U.S. Forest Service. At the visitor center, Pablo and his little brother Andrés learn that the forest has 240 kinds of native trees. Twenty-six of these are found nowhere else in the world. Some trees are more than 2,000 years old. In the lowest part of the forest, some trees are over 120 feet tall. On the highest mountain slopes, the trees are about 12 feet tall.

Many kinds of animals live in this rain forest. One is a tiny tree frog called the *coquí*. The name comes from the sound these frogs make: "koh-KEE, koh-KEE." El Yunque is also home to the endangered Puerto Rican parrot and to earthworms as long as baseball bats. Boas as long as cars roam the forest. Luckily, these snakes are not dangerous to humans.

The children at Culebra School are learning about the turtles and about other animals and plants on their island. Amanda and Neysha are fifth graders. They are examining a flower called a *canario* that blooms in many parts of Puerto Rico. They also peek into the flower of a cotton plant that grows wild by the school fence.

Amanda (left) *and Neysha* (right) *in science class in their school in Dewey, the main town on Culebra*

In class, the students discuss their feelings about tourists. Many tourists come to Puerto Rico to swim or snorkel. Some children don't like the way tourists leave trash on the beach. Other children would rather have the tourists than the U.S. Navy. U.S. Navy ships and planes are using the nearby island of Vieques for target practice. In the past, the navy used Culebra for target practice. Many Puerto Ricans want the navy to stop firing bombs at Vieques. They were glad in June 2001 when President George W. Bush announced plans to stop the bombing.

Rebecca (left) and Neysha (right) think this beach is one of the most beautiful places on Culebra. During the summer, Rebecca helps children with special needs learn about water safety and other skills.

Rebecca and Neysha sit atop an old army tank that was once used for target practice by the U.S. Navy.

Another dry part of Puerto Rico is the southwestern coast of the main island. This area is called Cabo Rojo ("Red Cape"). Many kinds of cacti grow in Cabo Rojo National Wildlife Refuge. Mangrove forests fringe the shoreline. A mangrove forest is one of the "crabbiest" places in the world. Thousands of crabs scurry around the base of these trees. Mangrove trees have odd, stiltlike roots. The roots mostly grow above ground.

Left, above: *Trees that grow on the dry, southwestern coast of Puerto Rico can live without much water.* Left, below: *Many kinds of cacti thrive in the area.* Above: *Mangrove forests grow near the shore.*

Not far from Cabo Rojo is the town of Sabana Grande. Narlyn goes often to Sabana Grande to visit her Aunt Abigail. Narlyn likes to dance. She would like to become a dancer and singer like Giselle, a Puerto Rican pop star. Two of Narlyn's favorite dances are merengue and salsa, which began in Puerto Rico and other islands of the West Indies.

Narlyn (left) *would like to become a dancer and singer like Giselle, a Puerto Rican pop star. Her younger sister, Christine* (right), *likes to dance, too.*

The people of Sabana Grande are having a week of celebrations called the *fiesta patronales* (festival of the patron saints). Many Catholics believe that patron saints look after them. Most towns in Puerto Rico have a patron saint.

Sabana Grande's patron saint is San Isidro Labrador, a farmer who lived in Spain in the 1100s. Since many people in Sabana Grande were once sugarcane farmers, they chose a farmer as a patron saint. Sugarcane is no longer a major crop in Puerto Rico. Most people in Sabana Grande work for businesses like the Pepsi distribution center and a local medical supply company. But the *fiesta patronales* is still an important tradition.

The *fiesta patronales* lasts for ten nights. Food stands serve everything from pizza to pork rinds. Children go on carnival rides, and their parents play a special horse race game called *pica*.

Gabriel's family has lived in Sabana Grande for many generations. His great-grandmother was a girl when U.S. warships landed on Puerto Rico at Guánica. Gabriel has often heard how

Above: *At Sabana Grande's fiesta, miniature horses race in a game called* pica. Right: *Children ride the merry-go-round. Some of the bands at the fiesta, like Grupomania, are world famous.*

Left: *Every year, many towns in Puerto Rico hold a festival like this one to honor their patron saint.* Above: *Gabriel would like to teach history someday.*

his great-grandmother saw U.S. soldiers ride into Sabana Grande on big horses. The soldiers were nice to the children and gave them food, clothes, and horseback rides.

Gabriel says Puerto Ricans were glad when the U.S. soldiers arrived. Many Puerto Ricans were tired of being a colony of Spain and wanted to govern themselves. Over the years, Puerto Ricans have

debated whether they want to be an independent nation, a U.S. state, or a U.S. commonwealth. In an election in 1998, Puerto Ricans voted to remain a commonwealth.

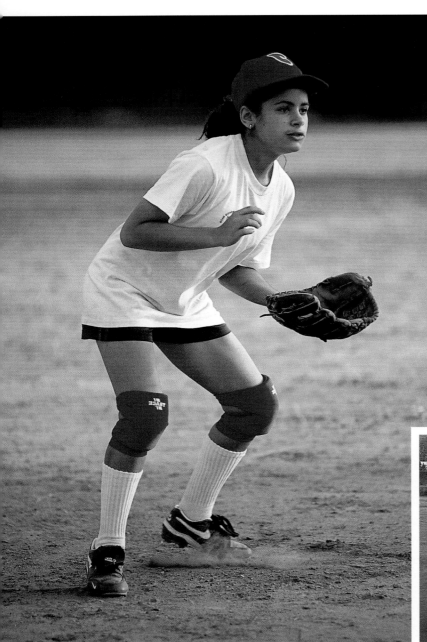

In the mountains north of Sabana Grande is the small town of Maricao. The air is cooler here than in the towns down by the sea. The Taínas, a girls softball team, is busy practicing softball. The team and their coach, Jose Lebron, are especially proud of Edalys, who plays third base, and Romary, a pitcher. They were picked for this year's Puerto Rican girls all-star team. Jose's daughter inspired both girls. She played on the Puerto Rican Olympic softball team in 1996. The team was the fourth best in the world. Both Edalys and Romary would like to represent

Edalys (above) *and her team, the Taínas* (right), *practice softball three times a week. Many of the girls started playing when they were about 11 years old.*

Puerto Rico in the Olympics someday.

A few miles from Maricao, Jadinar and Janira live on their small family farm, or *finca*. Their house is perched on a hillside. It is so remote that the family uses a generator for electricity. Sometimes they use their car to power the TV. Jadinar, who is in third grade, is lucky she has a sister, because no other children live nearby. A cousin lives way up the road, too far away for the girls to walk to.

Janira and Jadinar live near this remote hillside. Getting from place to place can be slow in Puerto Rico, since many roads are steep and winding.

When Jadinar and Janira first moved to the *finca,* it was covered by forest. Their father cut down the trees and planted coffee bushes, banana trees, and other crops. The coffee bushes produce bright red berries that are ready to pick in the fall.

Sometimes the girls help their parents with the harvesting. The work is hard because the hills are so steep. Coffee is the most important crop in Maricao, and each year the people hold a special festival to celebrate the harvest.

In 1998, most of the coffee crop was destroyed by a strong storm called Hurricane George. A severe hurricane occurs in Puerto Rico about once every 10 years. When Janira's family heard Hurricane George was on its way, the family left their house. They drove to their

The berries from these coffee trees will be dried and roasted before being sold as coffee beans. Where Janira and Jadinar live, the air is often fragrant with the rich odor of roasting coffee.

The ancient Taíno people played a ceremonial ball game called *batey*. Teams of 10 to 30 players had to keep a ball in the air without using their hands. A victory was thought to bring good health and a rich harvest.

Angel's church group visits Caguana. These stones have carvings of village chiefs, fertility gods, and other figures.

On the other side of the mountains from ancient Caguana is a very modern place, the Arecibo Observatory. It is dedicated to exploring outer space. The observatory has the world's largest radio telescope. A huge reflector dish catches radio waves from outer space. Radar photos taken here show faraway details, like volcanoes on Venus and ice on Mercury. The observatory uses special computers to analyze 168 million signals from space every few seconds. So far, none of the signals has been from extraterrestrial creatures.

Geovanny and his father have driven many miles to see the observatory. In the visitor center is a giant model that shows how the real telescope works. Outside, Geovanny and his dad look at the large reflector dish. Geovanny is happy he finally convinced his father to bring him here. Geovanny would like to study science at the University of Puerto Rico someday.

Opposite page: *Geovanny at the visitor center in Arecibo.* Right: *Geovanny's dad explains how the radio telescope at Arecibo helps scientists view different sections of space.*

Above: *These odd-shaped hills near Arecibo are made of limestone.* Right: *Yajaira (left) and David (third from left) live near the Arecibo Observatory.*

Yajaira and David can see the observatory from their house. They would both like to go to outer space someday. The limestone rock around their home has eroded into odd-shaped hills and deep, circular depressions. The huge reflector dish at the Arecibo Observatory was built in one of these depressions.

Both of Gilberto's parents work at the University of Puerto Rico's campus in Rio Piedras, a suburb of San Juan. The family lives in an apartment on the campus. Gilberto, who wants to be a lawyer someday, likes to walk around the campus. He and his friends like to watch NBA teams on television. Basketball is almost as popular as baseball in Puerto Rico.

Above: *Gilberto and his family live on the campus of the University of Puerto Rico.* Left: *Gilberto and his mother walk through the campus.*

Also on campus is a preschool that Ricardo and Valerie attend. All the children in their class are deaf. Ricardo and Valerie are learning sign language (a way of talking with hand signals). During recess, they have fun running around a play area with a large banyan tree in the center.

Ricardo and Valerie's class is just one part of a special school run by the University of Puerto Rico. The teachers experiment with new and exciting ways of teaching students from the early grades through high school. Children from all over San Juan apply to attend the school.

Above: Ricardo gets a piggyback ride around a huge banyan tree. Right: Valerie climbs up a slide. Opposite page: Valerie on the playground. Like the other children in her class, Valerie is learning sign language.

Above: *Two flute players.*
Right: *Students get ready to perform for family and friends.*

Music is important in Puerto Rico and at the school. It is hosting a concert in the beautiful old University Theater. Bands from the elementary, middle, and high school are performing. All the bands play a variety of music: show tunes, movie themes, rock and roll, and traditional Puerto Rican compositions.

The day after the concert, students come into class dripping wet from a downpour. Once they dry off, their art lesson begins. Ileana is mixing colors with acrylic paints. Other students are finishing paintings they started the week before. The art lessons combine with history and geography. The students say their combined art, history, and geography program makes them feel as if they are traveling around the world and through time.

Studying history (above) *and art* (below) *are both important in this Puerto Rican school.*

Below: *Angelica's teacher looks at one of Angelica's drawings.* Right: *Angelica and her* santo

Recently, the sixth graders learned about special figures made in Puerto Rico called *santos*. *Santos* represent Catholic saints and can be made of wood, clay, or other materials. Angelica enjoyed assembling a *santo*.

But she likes drawing even more. One year she won a medallion from the United Nations for a picture based on the Bible. The picture traveled with an exhibit to Spain.

The children of Puerto Rico live on a small island. But its contributions are great. Like other Puerto Rican children, the students in this classroom are discovering that Puerto Rico has a lot to give to its children and to the world around it.

44

Pronunciation Guide

Cabo Rojo   KAH-boh ROH-hoh
Caguana   KAHG-wahn-a
canario   ka-NAH-ryo
cemis   seh-MEES
conches   KAHN-chays
Loíza   loh-EE-sah
Maricao   mahr-ih-KOW
merengue   mah-REHN-gay
plátanos   PLA-ta-nos
Sabana Grande   sah-BAH-nah GRAHN-day
San Juan   SAHN HWAHN

Index

African people, 9, 12, 16
Animals, 20, 22–23, 26
Architecture, 13
Art lessons, 43–44
Arecibo Observatory, 36–38

Bananas, 14, 32
Baseball, 18–19

Cabo Rojo, 26
Cabo Rojo National Wildlife Refuge, 26
Caguana Indian Ceremonial Park,
    34–35
Caribbean National Forest, 20, 21
Celebrations, 16, 28
Cemis, 34
Climate, 17, 19, 22, 26
Coffee, 9, 32
Columbus, Christopher, 6, 8
Commonwealth status, 11, 29
Coquí, 20, 21
Culebra, 22–25
Culebra National Wildlife Refuge, 22

Dancing, 27

El Morro, 6, 10
El Yunque, 19–21

Families, 9, 14–15, 17, 22, 32, 39
Farming, 9, 28, 31–32

Firefighting, 22
Food, 14–15, 17, 28
Forts, 6, 10

Geology, 38
Giselle, 27
Gold, 8–9
Golf, 21

History, 6, 7–11, 28–29, 34–35
Hurricanes, 12, 32–33

Jobs, 14, 28, 32, 33

Language, 12, 18, 34
Location, 6
Loíza, 16
Luquillo, 21

Map, 7
Maricao, 30
Money, 15
Music, 13, 27, 28, 34, 42

Old San Juan, 13
Olympics, 30–31

Patron saints, 28, 29
Pirates, 10
Plants, 15, 20, 23, 26, 32

Puerto Rico, naming of, 8; population
    of, 12; size of, 6

Rainfall, 19
Rain forests, 19–21
Religion, 13, 16, 28, 34–35, 44

Sabana Grande, 27–29
San Juan, 6, 9, 10, 13, 34
Santos, 44
Schools, 23, 34, 40, 42–44
Slaves, 9, 12, 16
Softball, 30–31
Spain, 6, 11, 28, 29, 44
Spanish-American War, 11
Spanish culture, 12, 13; explorers, 6,
    8; military, 10; settlers, 9
Sports, 17, 21, 24, 39
Sugarcane, 9, 28

Taíno people, 6, 8–9,12, 34–35
Tourists, 24

United States, 11; Puerto Ricans in, 21
University of Puerto Rico, 37, 39
U.S. citizenship, 12
U.S. military, 24, 25, 29

Virgin Islands, 22

West Indies, 8, 27

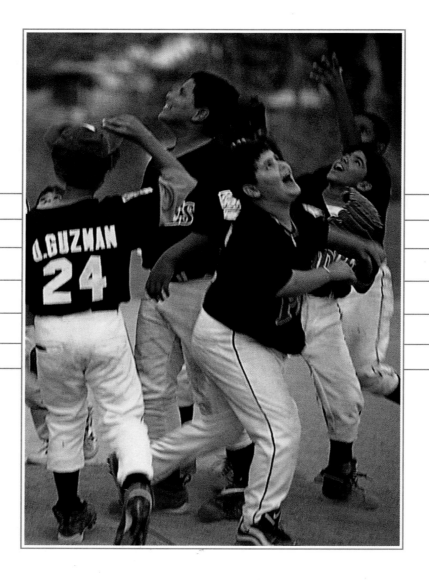